ART ATTACK™

Cracking New Year

CONTENTS

First published in 1999 by
Mammoth, an imprint of
Egmont Children's Books Limited,
239 Kensington High Street,
London W8 6SA

Christmas Cracker
Pages 2-9 © 1999 The Media Merchants,
Page 10 © 1999 Egmont Children's Books

Cracking New Year
Pages 2-10 © 1999 Egmont Children's Books,
Templates © 1999 Egmont Children's Books

Illustrations by Charlotte Stowell
Artwork photography
Christmas Cracker pages 3, 9, 10;
Cracking New Year pages 3, 5, 7-10
by Simon Russell

© & TM The Media Merchants TV Co. Ltd.
licensed by LMI

ISBN 0 7497 4002 7

1 2 3 4 5 6 7 8 9 10

Printed in Great Britain

Mammoth

Perfect Papier Mâché

Many of the projects in this book need papier mâché.

1

NEIL'S TIP
You can get PVA glue from any art supplies shop and most large stationery stores.

Pour some PVA glue into a bowl, then add half as much water. Stir them together to make a really strong mixture.

2

NEIL'S TIP
Make sure you protect your work surface with some old newspaper. If you work on a plastic bag you can simply peel off your project.

Coat the item in the glue mixture, and cover it in strips of newspaper or toilet roll. You will probably need two or three layers.

3

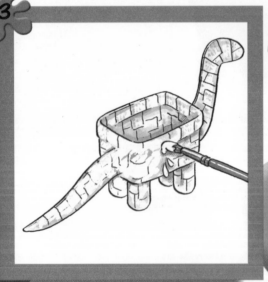

Then paint over everything again with the glue mixture, and leave it to dry.

Shiny Shaker

A fantastic Art Attack for your left-over party plates.
(Make sure they're clean!)

1 Make sure your paper plates are clean, then paint the backs of the two plates in bright colours. Leave to dry.

2 Cut some strips of tissue paper or ribbon, and tape them to the inside of one of the plates.

3 Place a handful of dried beans in the same plate and spread some glue around the edge. Carefully place the other plate face down on top of the first.

4 Tape all round the edge and paint over it. Add more decoration using foil, shapes cut from wrapping paper, sweet wrappers and even sequins.

Now just shake and shine!

3

Flashy Feathere

WHAT YOU NEED
plastic bottle (1 litre), small balloon, sticky tape, thick paper, scissors, PVA glue, pencil, papier mâché, 2 plastic bottle tops, paint, parcel ribbon

This is a brilliant way of using up all those empty plastic bottles.

1

Pour something into the bottle to act as a weight and stop it falling over. Sand is ideal, or you could use dried beans or peas.

Blow up the balloon until it is about the size of a large orange. Tape it to the neck of the bottle.

3

Draw round a small plate on to the paper and divide it in half to make a semi-circle. Cut this out, roll it into a cone and tape it in position as a beak. Glue on the bottle tops as the eyes.

4

Cover the head and bottle in several layers of papier mâché. Leave to dry overnight.

5

Cut 2 wings and 2 feet from thick paper, gluing them to the bottle. Paint the bird bright colours. You could also glue on shapes cut from wrapping paper.

6

Make some ribbon curls by pulling strips of parcel ribbon against the side of a closed pair of scissors. Glue them to the head.

WAX CRAYON

Funky Frames

Show off your favourite photos in these stunning frames.

WHAT YOU NEED
cardboard box, ruler, pencil, scissors, masking tape, paint, tissue paper, glue, thin card, sticky tack, string, sticky tape

Cut the side off the cardboard box. Cut out 2 strips 18cm long and 4cm wide, and 2 strips 10cm long and 4cm wide.

Stick the strips together with masking tape to make a frame.

Stick some masking tape along the inside and outside edges of the frame. Paint over the edges of the frame and leave to dry.

Tear up lots of small squares of tissue paper and roll them into balls. Working on one bit at a time, cover the frame with glue and stick the balls close together until the frame is full.

5

NEIL'S TIP
A safe way to make holes in cardboard is to push the point of a hard pencil through it into some sticky tack.

Cut out a piece of thin card slightly smaller than your frame. This will be your backing. Make two holes in the card. Thread a loop of string through and tie a knot.

6

Place the frame face down. Tape your photo or picture in position, then tape the backing card over the top.

NEIL'S TIP
You can use wrapping paper for this - or even shiny sweet wrappers.

You could also...

• Create a mosaic effect with tiny squares of wrapping paper.
• Stick layers of different-coloured tissue paper down for a multi-coloured effect.

Surprise Thank Yous

Surprise all your friends and relations with these unique thank you cards.

WHAT YOU NEED
old wrapping paper, pencil, scissors, glue, thin card, parcel ribbon

1 Draw a stocking shape on to some wrapping paper and cut it out. Turn the stocking over and glue all round the edge, but NOT along the top.

2 Fold the card in half and stick the stocking on to the front, leaving some space at the top.

3 Cut a rectangle of card and fold it in half. It should be just small enough to sit in the top of the stocking. Glue some wrapping paper on to one side of the card.

Fill the stocking with your special surprise thank you.

4 Glue some ribbon and a thank you tag on to the mini parcel, then write your message inside.

Rainbow Thank Yous

Write your thank you letters on this fantastic "designer" stationery.

WHAT YOU NEED
thin card, A4 paper, wax crayons, pencil, thick brush or pen

1 Scribble on to the card with the wax crayons. Use lots of different colours and completely cover the card.

2 Turn the card face down on top of the clean sheet of paper. Very lightly draw a pattern on the back of the card.

3 Now rub over the pencil lines firmly with the end of a thick brush or pen. Hold the card very still while you do this.

4 Peel back the card, to reveal your rainbow design.

thank you!

You can use this technique for all sorts of letters and stationery all year round.

Dishy Dinos

Clear up your clutter, or store your sweets, in one of these great dinosaur dishes.

WHAT YOU NEED
pencil, card, rectangular margarine tub, sticky tape, kitchen roll or tissue paper, papier mâché, paint

1

Trace the dinosaur head and tail on to a piece of card folded in half. Cut them out to give you 2 heads and 2 tails.

2

Fold the ends of the heads and tails then tape them on to the margarine tub.

3

Cut out 4 strips of card. Roll them into tubes and tape them to the bottom of the tub.

4

Add some scrunched-up kitchen roll or tissue paper to give a more 3D effect, then cover the whole thing in several layers of papier mâché. Leave to dry overnight.

5

Paint your dinosaur in bright colours and leave it to dry. Then give it another coat of PVA glue and leave it to dry again to make it really shiny.

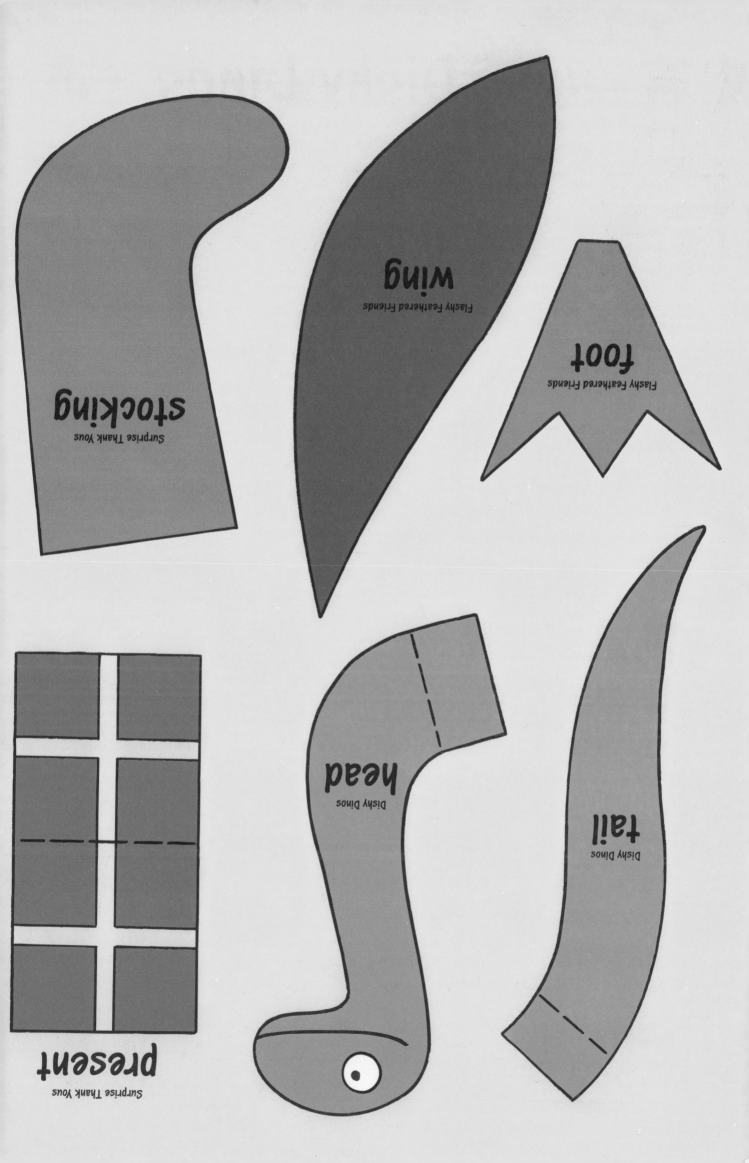

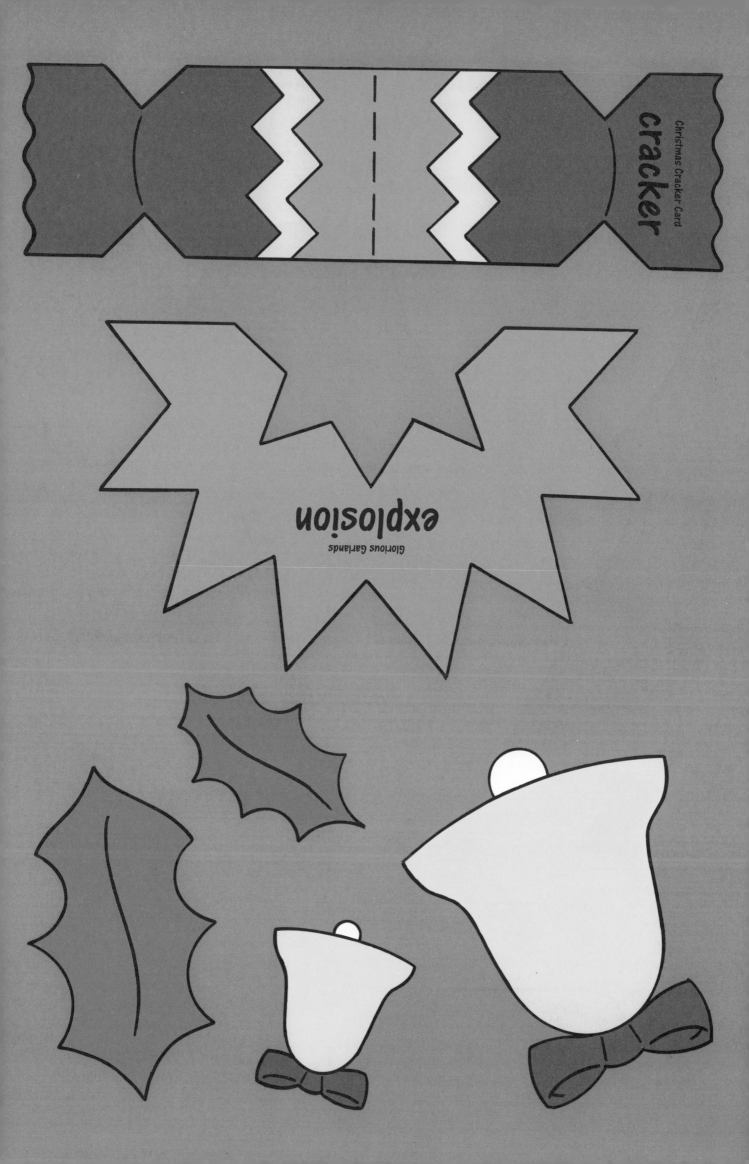

Christmas Cracker Card

cracker

explosion

Glorious Garlands

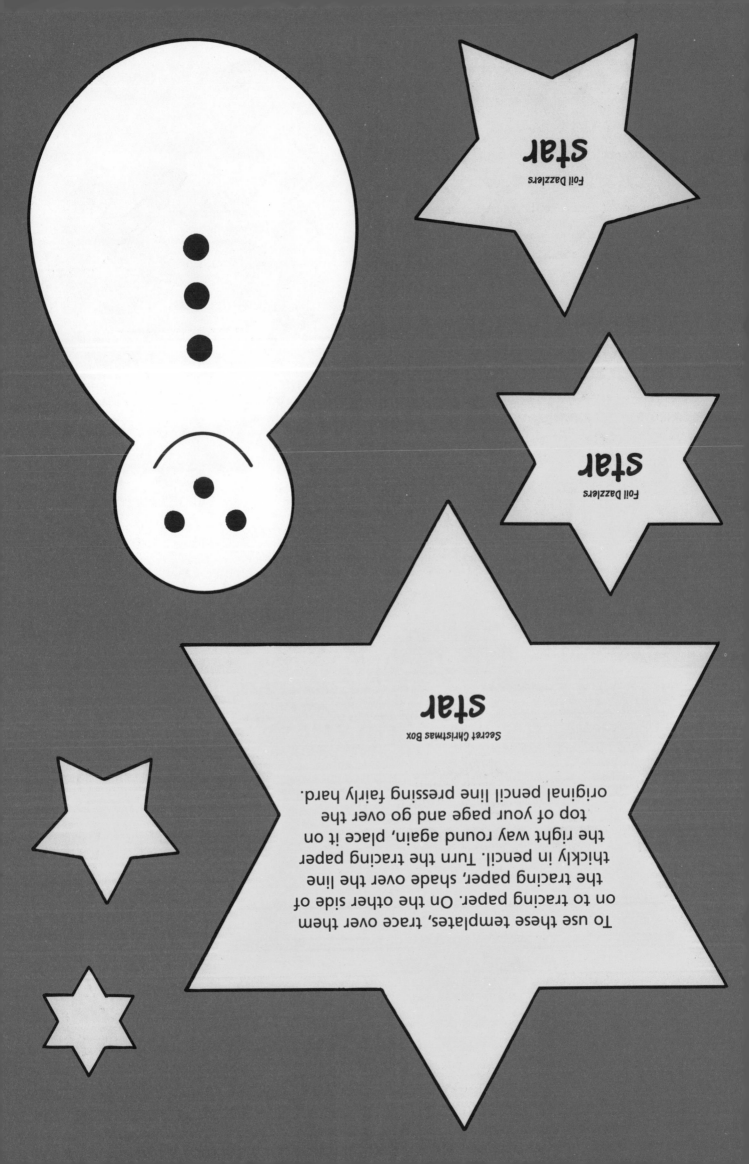

star

Foil Dazzlers

star

Foil Dazzlers

star

Secret Christmas Box

To use these templates, trace over them on to tracing paper. On the other side of the tracing paper, shade over the line thickly in pencil. Turn the tracing paper the right way round again, place it on top of your page and go over the original pencil line pressing fairly hard.

Foil Dazzlers

These fancy foil decorations will look fantastic on your Christmas tree.

WHAT YOU NEED

card, large mug, pencil, scissors, PVA glue, string, foil, acrylic paint, sponge, ribbon

1 Draw round the mug on to the card twice, and cut out the circles.

2 Draw a Christmas design on to each of the circles then cover the pencil lines with PVA glue.

3 Leave the glue until it is tacky then stick down some string along the lines of your design. Add some foil balls.

4 Wrap a piece of foil over each of the circles. Press it down gently over the string and fold over the back. Lightly sponge some paint on to the foil.

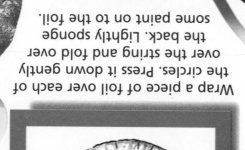

5 Glue the back of both circles then stick them together with a loop of ribbon in the middle so you can hang it up.

Just hang it on your tree and watch it sparkle in the Christmas lights.

When dry, carefully
pull the garland
out to display it.

5

Place another star on top and this time
glue both sides.

6

Repeat placing stars and gluing alternately
top-and-bottom and side-to-side until all the
stars are used up. Leave to dry.

Glorious Garlands

Brighten up your room with these dazzling Christmas decorations.

WHAT YOU NEED
5 sheets of different coloured paper (A3 size), pencil, scissors, glue

1

Fold one of the sheets of paper in half 3 times.

2

Position the paper with the folded edge at the bottom and draw a zig-zag explosion.

3

Cut away the shaded area to make 4 stars. Repeat with the other 4 sheets of paper, to make 20 stars all together.

4

Take one star and dab some glue at the top and the bottom.

5 Score along the lines again and fold back each half.

6 Draw a cracker design across the front of the card, and paint it bright colours. Leave to dry.

7 Cut away the card around the cracker.

8 Open out the card and design your Christmas message inside. Add finishing touches with gold or silver pen.

HAVE A CRACKING CHRISTMAS

Christmas Cracker Card

Give everyone a cracker of a Christmas with this unique Art Attack Christmas Card!

WHAT YOU NEED
A4 sheet of thin card, scissors, pencil, ruler, paint, gold or silver pen

1
Cut the sheet of card in half lengthways. Then divide one half into three equal sections.

2
Use a pair of closed scissors to score down the pencil lines, pressing firmly against the ruler.

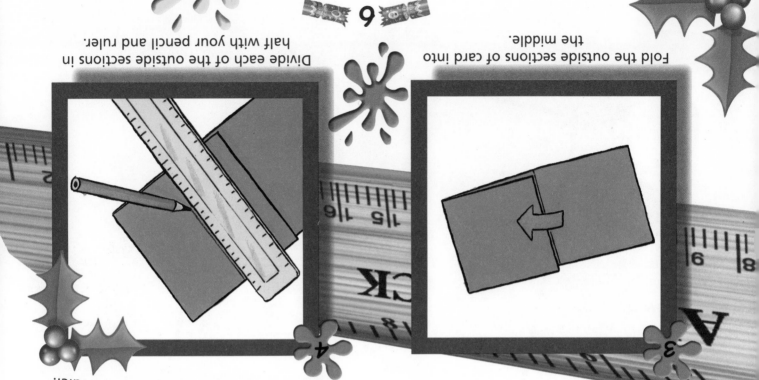

3
Fold the outside sections of card into the middle.

4
Divide each of the outside sections in half with your pencil and ruler.

5

Fill the jar up to the neck with cold, clean water.

6

Pour a quarter of a tube of glitter into the water. Give it a stir, then screw the lid on firmly.

NEIL'S TIP
Don't fill the jar right up the top – just up to the neck to leave a little air space.

Just turn the jar upside down for a fantastic Christmas glitter shower.

Santa Glitter Shakers

There's nothing like a bit of glitter to put you in a Christmassy mood.

1

Take the lid off the jar and cover the outside of the lid in glue.

2

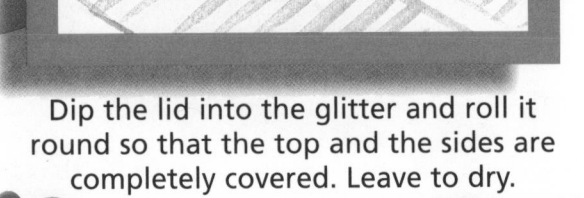

Dip the lid into the glitter and roll it round so that the top and the sides are completely covered. Leave to dry.

3

Roll some white modelling clay into a ball about the size of a golf ball and press it on to the inside of the lid. Leave enough room round the edge so that the lid can be screwed back on to the jar.

4

Sprinkle some glitter on to the modelling clay and press down any loose flakes. Push the cake decoration into the modelling clay.

6

Paint the whole box, false bottom and lid and leave to dry. Paint bright Christmas patterns over the box and the lid – don't forget the inside of the box and the back of the lid. Leave to dry, then add highlights in gold and silver pen.

NEIL'S TIP
A safe way to make holes in cardboard is to push the point of a sharp pencil through it into some sticky tack.

7

Make two holes in the back of the box and two more in the lid. Make sure they line up. Thread some ribbon through the holes to attach the lid to the box.

8

Cut two strips of ribbon about 15cm long. Cut two star shapes out of card and stick them on to the front of the box and the lid to hold the ribbon ties in place. Add a 'Keep out' warning to keep any snoopers away.

You can use this all year round. Just redecorate it and use it to keep all your secrets in.

3

Secret Christmas Box

Before Christmas, hide everyone's presents in the secret compartment. After Christmas, keep your own favourite gifts safe there.

1

Cut the top flaps off the smaller box. Cut the two larger sides off the larger box.

WHAT YOU NEED
2 cardboard grocery boxes (one slightly larger than the other), scissors, pencil, ruler, PVA glue, papier mâché, paint, silver and gold pens, ribbon, thin card

2

lid

false bottom

Draw round the smaller box on to each of the other two pieces of cardboard. Cut one of these just inside your pencil line (so that it fits easily inside the smaller box). Cut the other just outside your pencil line (so that it sits on top of the smaller box).

3

Cut the two shorter sides off the larger box. On each piece, measure and draw a line down the middle. Then draw another line one ruler's width away from this, and a third line one ruler's width from the far edge. Score down each of these lines with scissors taped shut for safety.

4

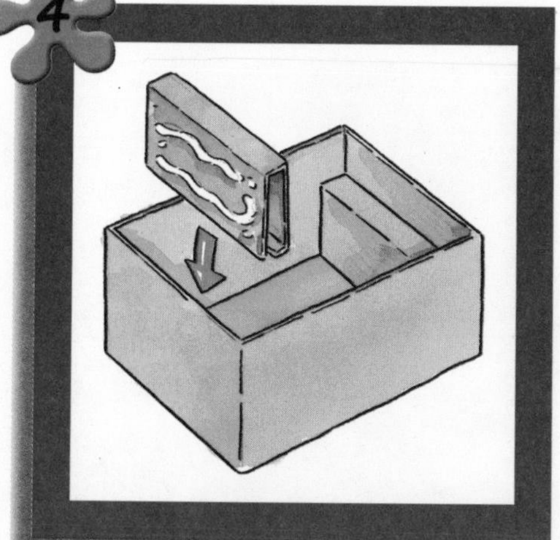

Fold the pieces of cardboard and stick them inside the box.

5

Cover the box, the false bottom and the lid with papier mâché. Leave to dry overnight. (Flip the book to find Perfect Papier Mâché on page 2.)

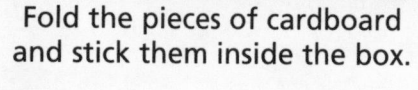

ART ATTACK ™

Christmas Cracker

CONTENTS

WARNING
Be very careful when using sharp objects, such as scissors.

This pencil symbol means that there is a template in the centre 4 pages of the book to help you with your Art Attack.

This clock symbol means that you have to leave your Art Attack to dry, often overnight.

WAX CRAYON

mammoth